TH
BO

THE RAG AND BONE BOY

SUSAN HOLLIDAY

The Rag and Bone Boy
LD693F
ISBN 1 85503 153 1
© Susan Holliday
© cover Ted Lazlo Design
All rights reserved
First published 1992

LDA, Duke Street, Wisbech, Cambs, PE13 2AE

1

My Friend Jack

Mr Barker once shouted so hard his teeth nearly fell out. It was Tuesday, Midsummer Day – the day when it all began.

'Rubbish! Total rubbish!' Mr Barker held up Jack's English homework book.

'Complete rubbish. Don't you ever listen, Jack Dobbin?'

Jack didn't answer.

'Deaf as well?' shouted Mr Barker. His black hair stuck out with anger. His big white teeth shook. We waited for them to slip out and fall into his lap. They did once before when Jack gave in a mega-inkblot for his homework.

Silence.

'Jack is a little deaf, sir,' I said, trying to be helpful.

'Who do you think you are, Charlie Williams?' shouted Mr Barker.

There didn't seem to be a good reply so I was silent as well.

At last Jack spoke. 'I do listen, sir,' he said calmly. 'It's my mum, sir.'

Mr Barker shook.

'Using your mother as an excuse, eh?'

'No, sir. You see, she's a rag-and-bone man and...'

We all laughed. All except Amy. She never laughed at Jack.

Jack always called his mum a rag-and-bone man. Perhaps it was in memory of his dad. They used to go all over England with the other travellers, but after they settled in the cottage his dad started the round. Jack told me the travellers were used to that sort of work. One day his dad walked out and Jack's mum took over the round. Everyone in our town knows her.

'Don't be funny with me!' said Mr Barker. We watched his teeth carefully as he shouted again.

'You can stay in and do your work WELL.'

'I will do it again,' said Jack, 'but I can't stay in.'

'That's enough,' shouted Mr Barker. He threw the book at Jack and began to write 'HOMEWORK' on the board. The chalk was squeaky.

I could tell Mr Barker was very angry indeed. When he is calm his writing is clear and upright. It is the best writing I have ever seen. That day it was almost lying down. As if Mr Barker was having a fit or something.

'You're in for it,' I said to Jack when school was over.

'I know,' said Jack. 'But my mum's sick. We need the money. Yesterday I cleared a house. Today I have to do the round before it's dark.'

'Not to worry,' I said, 'it's 24 June. The longest day in the year.'

'You always know things,' said Jack.

In a way that was true. That is why Jack and I stuck together. And Amy too. We were a bit different from the others. In class the three of us sat in the back row. Jack and I were the Long and the Short. Jack was big and strong. He was much older than the rest of us. I was just 13 and small and thin. But it was not me they call Short. It was Jack. You see, he was meant to be short on brains. The fact that he knew all about birds and could whistle like them didn't count. Jack always came last in class, and I always came top. As for Amy, she was Sri Lankan and her dad wouldn't let her go out with boys. All the other girls go out with boys all the time. Once Amy did go out, with this sixth-former. He was a real swot and wore glasses and played the violin. Her dad was angry when he found out but her mum was kinder. Her mum was more like a sister. They often shopped together and looked for good buys.

'My mum says you're not like boys,' Amy once told us. We didn't hit her. We knew she meant we wouldn't date her. She was dead right. Mind you, she seemed to like Jack. When she walked home with us she was always next to him.

That afternoon her mum came for her in the big car. 'There's a rug sale,' she told us with a smile, so Jack and I walked home without her.

'Shark's teeth means business,' I said to Jack. 'Did you see his writing? Do you want me to do that work for you?'

Jack's smile lit up his light brown face. I wondered if he looked like his dad.

'I could forge your handwriting,' I said.

We sat on the pavement and looked at his book. It was very bad. Worse than I had thought. As if no one had ever taught him to make letters. No wonder Mr Barker shouted at him.

Jack smiled again. He always had great faith in me.

'Thanks. You see, I haven't the time, what with

Mum and the round. Why don't you come in for a Coke?'

It was his way of saying thank you.

'Jack lived a mile out of town, near where they were building the council estate. His cottage was small and dark. It smelled damp and old. Everywhere was piled up with boxes and bundles wrapped in newspaper. There were old clothes smelling of mothballs. Junk was everywhere, on the floor, on the table, on the chairs, even on the cooker. Herbs were everywhere too, dried in bottles or hanging in bunches from rusty hooks.

I was shocked. My mum and dad don't like me to leave anything about. Not even myself. I have to do my homework in the bedroom away from the TV. Seen and not heard, that's me. No wonder I come top of the class.

'JACK... JACK...'

We went into his mother's bedroom. I was used to seeing Jack's mum on her round – a big lady in a pink scarf. She drove her pony and cart as if she were in the Wild West.

Now her brown eyes were dull, her black hair hung loose, her hands were limp. She drank something green from a green glass and pulled herself up.

'Someone was snooping round here today,' she

said. 'He was at the window so I stuck my tongue out.' She cackled and the gaps between her teeth showed.

'That scared him off! Always frighten them off, Jack.'

I can't imagine Jack scaring anyone off. He is the softest boy I know.

'Do you want anything, Mum?' he said.

She said 'No' and nodded at the glass.

'This will pull me through the fever.'

We had our Cokes and went round the back. Although they were building lots of council houses they hadn't touched the little field at the bottom of Jack's tiny garden.

'Not for want of trying,' said Jack, 'but Mum sticks up for us.'

The little field was crowded. There was Polly the pony, an old cart and two broken-down sheds.

'That shed belongs to me,' said Jack, pointing to the one on the right.

'Why do you have a shed?' I asked.

'For my secret things,' he said. 'I'm the only one with a key.'

In the other shed were a bale of hay and a harness hanging over a rusty hook on the wall. Jack took it down and harnessed Polly to the old cart. He led the pony round to the side of the cottage and tied her up to a post. We began to load up the cart. By now it was getting late.

'I'll go your way,' said Jack, 'but first let's have a piece of bread and cheese. I'm too hungry to wait.'

I followed him back inside. The place was a little clearer now but there was still a lot of junk about. Jack opened the fridge and I went to the sink for some water. I stood by the sink and looked up at the window.

I froze with horror. A face was pressed to the pane. The eyes were red-rimmed and blue, the skin was yellow. The hair was wild and grey. The face did not look real. It was more like something I thought up when Mum and Dad were at the pictures and I suddenly got scared. It was a face that was out to get something. Or someone.

I turned to Jack. He was still looking for his cheese. When I turned back again, the face had gone.

2

The Old Box

'What's the matter?' said Jack, putting a large lump of cheese and a big loaf on the table.

He began to saw the bread with something that looked like a huge butcher's knife.

Perhaps I should not tell him about the face. Perhaps I imagined it. Mum said I had too much imagination. Yet I always told Jack everything. He was that sort of friend. So I took a mouthful of bread and cheese and told him about the face at the window, with red-rimmed eyes and yellow skin. The sight of Jack's knife set me off again. 'The face of a killer, perhaps!'

'It's the snooper,' said Jack, so calmly I almost felt a fool. He cut another lump of bread and held up the gleaming knife. 'Mum saw him. Maybe someone's playing a joke.'

'It didn't look like a joke to me,' I said, copying

The Old Box

Jack and eating off the table.

Jack smiled. 'Midsummer madness, then.'

He always gave people the benefit of the doubt. Soft in the head, my mother said.

The thought of my mum made me sweep the crumbs up into a little pile at the edge of the table. I looked round but there was nowhere to throw them away. But the sight of all that junk gave me another thought.

'The snooper might be after something,' I said. 'After all, you have all sorts of things here.'

'You can say that again,' said Jack, stuffing bread and cheese into his mouth. He stood up. 'Better get on.'

I followed him outside. I loved sitting beside Jack on the little seat in front of his trap.

'You must be the last rag-and-bone man in England,' I told him as we made our way down the road. 'My mum says it's all car boot sales nowadays.'

'We can't afford a car,' said Jack. 'Anyway, it's not true. A lot of travellers sell like us.'

'Not round here, they don't,' I said. 'You're famous, you and your mum.'

When I first became friends with Jack I found a book that said how some of the travellers had to be housed because things were too tough on the road. Perhaps that's why his dad had run off. Perhaps he hated living in a house and felt like jumping out of the window. My mind ran riot again, but even I wasn't up to dreaming up what I found in the back of the cart as Jack pulled up outside my house.

'Give me your work, then,' I said, but he couldn't find where he had put his homework. So while he held the reins I climbed on to the back of the cart and went through all the junk. It wasn't long before I came across an old box. Like everything else it looked as if it had seen better days. It was covered in tatty leather and the clasp was rusty. But it looked a lot more fun than Jack's homework so I opened it up.

Inside was a big book with beautiful drawings. There were flowers and herbs and shrubs, all with Latin names. I knew they were Latin names because I'm in the Latin class – the Roman Snobs group, the others call us. There was another book underneath, handwritten and all in Latin. It looked moth eaten. Jack turned round to look.

'I'll keep those books with my secret things,' he said. 'You can share them, Charlie.'

I jumped off the cart and at that moment my hand landed on his homework bag. It seemed like a reward I could give him and as he rode off I

The Old Box

shouted after him, 'I'll do my best to make it look just like yours.'

That night I tried to keep to my word. I had to work under the bedclothes by torch light. I didn't dare put the light on because my mum has a thing about early nights and would have stopped me dead in my tracks.

I was right. It wasn't easy, forging Jack's writing by torch light. The bedclothes kept getting in the way of the biro and once or twice I wrote on the sheets by mistake. The writing itself was strange – perhaps when Jack's family were on the road he never went to school. I knew people taught travellers but maybe he kept out of the way. Anyway, he did lots of other things, like collecting flowers and bird-songs and cigarette stubs (I was always trying to keep him off smoking). He knew lots of stories as well. He was even good at telling them. But as for reading and writing, he couldn't have bothered. I had a real struggle trying to copy his writing.

In the end it was all worthwhile. The next day Jack gave in his homework. Mr Barker bared his teeth, but it was more in sorrow than in anger.

On the way home, we told Amy all about the homework. She smiled and put on her big loopy earrings. Jack said if we liked we could both go home with him to have a look at the books.

When we arrived at Jack's house, he went indoors to see his mum while Amy and I went down to the shed. It didn't take me long to know someone had been prowling about.

First there was this library ticket lying in the grass. I was amazed. The last thing I expected to find was a library ticket. Then I looked at the padlock on the shed door.

'Someone's tried to get in,' I said to Amy.

She looked round. 'Why would someone prowl round here? The pony must be 101 and the shed looks like something out of the ark. You must know what I mean.'

I did know what she meant and decided to leave it at that. If I told her I'd seen the face of a killer at Jack's window, she would have given me that smile of hers, just to remind me I am a lot smaller and younger than she is.

Jack came down the field and looked very worried. 'We'd better not be long. My mum's quite ill. She needs me up there.'

He put the key in the padlock and I still didn't say anything. On top of everything else, I wasn't going to let him worry about my silly fears.

3

Jack's Shed

Jack's shed was like a down-market Aladdin's cave. On a long table under the window there was everything from pebbles to an old pair of boots.

'The ones my dad left behind,' Jack told us, as he lit up a cigarette stub. My mum would have moaned about passive smoking but I knew my lungs could take it. By the table there was a broken wooden rocking-chair. Behind the chair there was a pile of ragged leather cases and a big, old chest. Jack opened its stiff lid and took out the box.

We cleared the table and looked at the books together. Jack sat in his rocking-chair and Amy and I stood on either side.

'It's amazing what you pick up,' said Amy. 'Where did you get them from, Jack?'

'House clearance,' said Jack. 'Someone had died.'

'I don't suppose anyone had opened the box for ages,' I said.

Amy leaned forward. Her earrings dangled beside Jack's head.

'I love the drawings of plants.'

'Is it a nature book?' asked Jack.

Amy nodded and one of her earrings brushed his cheek. 'It must be.'

I turned the beautiful pages back to the beginning. 'I'm not sure,' I said, trying not to sound like a know-all, 'I think it's a herbal.'

'What's that?'

'You know – about herbs. Like your mum has.'

'For gardening?' Amy often helped her mother in the garden.

'I'm not sure. I'll look it up tonight,' I told them.

'It looks like it's worth a lot of money.'

'What about the notebook?' asked Amy.

'It doesn't look much,' I said. 'It's handwritten.'

It was very fragile and torn round the edges. It was all in Latin and seemed to be about a doctor and the way he cured his patients. It would not have been easy to read in English because the ink was faded and the letters looked odd. In Latin it was impossible. Even so, the letters were easier to read than Jack's.

'There might be something in it to help my mum,' said Jack, when I told him.

'That would be wonderful,' said Amy, leaning over Jack so that she could see the book.

'It's by someone called Dr John Hall,' I said.

Jack put the books carefully into the box.

'If only I could find a cure for my mum's fever.'

He put the box into the trunk. 'Don't forget, these are my secret things. Not a word to anyone!'

I have lived all my life with my World Dictionary (2,032 pages and 200,000 definitions). My mum bought it when I was 2 because I did a 100-piece jigsaw without thinking. I've never done a jigsaw since and the dictionary has always been a bit of a turn-off except for homework. Sometimes I sit with it open, to give my mum the right impression. I suppose I've learned quite a lot that way.

That evening I sat with it in front of the TV and thumbed my way through the h's. My mum looked at me lovingly.

'Can I help you, dear?' She probably could, being a teacher and a swot in her own right. But I wasn't going to risk it.

'It's OK, Mum.'

For all its information, my World Dictionary was no good on herbals so I spent my next lunch hour in the school library. Mr Barker came in to do his marking. He smiled at me as I took out a book called The Herbal Handbook. I looked at him from time to time. Suddenly he began to mutter and curse under his breath. It must have been Jack's homework.

Perhaps I had made too good a job of it.

'Someone should teach him to read and write,' he said, half to me. His eyes looked as if they were popping out on stalks.

'He does his best,' I said. I felt quite proud. Perhaps I had done a good job of copying Jack's writing.

At break I read a few quotes from The Herbal Handbook to Jack and Amy.

> *Doctors used to carry herbal recipes in little fold-up books. The books were kept in leather cases that dangled from their belts...*
>
> *Some doctors made up their own recipes...*
>
> *The powers of herbs cannot be denied...*

'That's what my mum says,' said Jack. 'Perhaps my books can help her. Could you come in on the way back and read to me?'

That evening Amy and I tried to help Jack. This time his herbal looked even more old and precious and the notebook by Dr John Hall looked even more fragile. I was frightened to turn the pages in case they tore. Then I found a piece of paper between the leaves of the notebook. It was an English translation of a cure for fever. I read it out.

'Maybe that's the cure I need,' said Jack excitedly. 'I wish I could read it myself.'

'No reason why you can't,' said Amy. I looked at her stunned. If Jack couldn't read *The Beano*, how on earth could he be expected to read this. It was then that I really looked hard at the decorated front page of the herbal.

I read:

THE HERBALL OR GENERAL HISTORY OF PLANTES GATHERED BY JOHN GERARDE OF LONDON IMPRINTED AT LONDON BY JOHN NORTON 1597

Jack took the book and followed the words.

'I'll help you,' said Amy. 'I always wanted to be a teacher.' She smiled at Jack.

'It's quite hard,' I said.

'Let's begin now,' said Amy. 'The drawings will help.'

'I'll copy some of those one day,' said Jack.

I went outside. I felt unhappy. How could Jack

learn to read from such a hard book? But then, he wanted to. He really wanted to. It might have the cure to his mother's illness. And if she got better he would have more time for his own work.

It was then that I saw the back of a figure running round the side of the cottage towards the gate. The man had a funny run, as if his body sloped to one side. He stopped for a moment and turned round. His face was yellow with red-rimmed eyes. It was Yellowface. I ran after him as fast as I could go. When I reached the gate I looked up and down the road. There was no one in sight. On the other side of the road a car was pulling away. For all I knew it belonged to the man in the house opposite. Pehaps I was dreaming again.

I decided to say nothing to Jack and Amy. I ran down the road as fast as I could go, just in case my mum thought I had been kidnapped. Her imagination was even wilder than mine, if that was possible!

4

Thief!

The next day Amy was going out with her mother, so Jack asked me if I would teach him to read the cures in the book. I said I could stay for ten minutes but that was all. My mum had told me not to be late again. It wasn't often I used my mother as an excuse.

'I haven't long myself,' said Jack. 'There was a phone call about a house clearance. They're moving and want it done quickly. It's in your road so I can take you home when I go.'

In the shed Jack showed me a copy of a yellow musk rose he had copied from Gerarde's Herball. I had no idea he could draw so well.

'You should do more,' I told him. 'You're miles better than me.'

As I expected, the reading lesson did not go so well. Jack only wanted to read the translation from the notebook. In the end there was so little time I read it to him.

Mrs Mary Herbert aged 45
Hecktick Feaver

The cure included everything from a herbal mixture to something called a caudle of yolks of eggs, wine and sugar. There were quite a lot of words I would have to look up. I thought it all sounded rather strange but Jack had a strong feeling it would help his mum.

'Later on I'll have a go at reading it on my own,' he said.

He put the books back into the box and into the chest. 'And I'll try to write it out,' he told me as we left.

I enjoyed the ride home. I got down at the house Jack was going to clear. To my surprise I knew it straightaway, No. 23. The house with the bright blue and orange door. It belonged to a friend of my mother's who said she was an artist, though you woudn't think so from her colour scheme. Jack went up to knock on the door and I waved goodbye.

'Rosie's house?' said Mum when I told her about No. 23. 'It can't be true. I met Rosie at the Do-It-Yourself only today. She never said she was moving.'

My mum frowned. 'Come to think of it, she was buying paint for the bathroom. Black,' she added gloomily.

'What were *you* doing there?' I asked.

My dad and I dread Mum going to the Do-It-Yourself shop. It spells trouble and temper. It spells change.

'Something must be done about the living-room,' said Mum. 'It's getting yellow.'

I sighed. I remembered the last time she decorated. Then it was the kitchen that was going yellow. My dad took to the garden and I locked myself in my bedroom. For days there was hardly any food. My dad and I got quite thin. In the end we went to McDonald's.

Mum looked at me sharply. Perhaps I was showing my feelings. But it was Rosie who was on her mind. 'Rosie likes black,' she said, as if her friend was mad. 'Fancy liking black. Must be a morbid streak. Funny person. Knows funny people. Arty.'

'It's strange Jack had that phone call from her,' I said. 'Perhaps she's painting the house to sell.'

'If she was moving she would tell me,' said my mum firmly.

I stamped upstairs and Mum shouted, 'Supper's ready,' so I stamped down again.

'Well, I hope it's not the last suppper,' I said. Or did I hope that? As I dipped my fork into the fish pie I thought about going to McDonald's. It was a lot more fun than my mum's carefully chosen meals. Perhaps Jack could come with us.

The next day Jack wasn't at school.

'Jack Dobbin,' called Mr Barker, his biro hovering over the register like a bird of prey.

'His mum's ill,' I said.

'So is my wife,' snarled Mr Barker. 'That doesn't stop *me* from coming to school.'

I reckoned living with Shark's teeth was enough to make anyone ill. I crossed my fingers under the desk.

'Jack's ill too. He has a fever.' I listed some of the terms from the cure. I wanted to blind him with science.

'Sounds as though he is on his deathbed,' said Mr Barker evenly, as he dug a cross next to Jack's name. I wondered why he hated Jack so much.

Thief!

Perhaps it was because Jack's family were travellers. I decided if ever I was Prime Minister I would make laws for travellers. I would let them go wherever they wanted. As my dad said, it's a free country.

All that day I was worried. By the time break arrived I had Jack tied up and thrown into the river by Yellowface.

I had his mum leaning out of the window calling his name and crying on her own. I had to talk to someone, so I spoke to Amy.

'Don't be silly,' she said, 'he's bunked off, that's all.'

'I don't believe it,' I said. 'He never bunks off. He wants to learn, whatever Shark's teeth thinks. Will you come round to his place with me?'

'No problem,' said Amy. 'My mum's at a tea-party.'

Later that day we knocked on Jack's door. There was no answer so we went round the back. The pony and trap were in place but the door to Jack's shed was swinging open. I went in, half expecting to see Jack on the floor. Instead everything was turned upside down. Pieces of glass were scattered on the floor. The ashtray was smashed. Jack's dad's boots had been thrown down any old how. Dried flowers were all over the place.

'It's Yellowface,' I said to Amy. 'I've seen him here twice already. Once at the window. Once in the garden. Now he's ruined everything.'

I was near to tears and Amy was very angry. 'Why should anyone do this to Jack?' she asked.

We ran round to the front of the cottage. There were rosemary bushes and meadowsweet and all the other herbs Jack's mum loves growing among buttercups. At least they were still in their place.

We knocked loudly and this time Jack came to the door. He looked ill.

'What's happened?' I asked.

'Someone broke in. They came for the books. They smashed everything. And that's not the worst of it.' He looked very sad.

'My mum's worse. I know she is. She heard the noise but could do nothing about it. It made her more feverish but she still won't let me call the doctor. I need to make up that cure for her but I can't remember it and the translation was with the books. Can you remember it Charlie?'

Jack sounded desperate, like someone who was clutching at straws.

Thief!

I knew I was famous for my brains, but a lot had happened since I read that cure out loud to Jack. It felt like a year ago, not like the afternoon before.

I sat at the kitchen table and put my hands over my eyes. The smell of dried herbs drifted over me but didn't refresh my memory.

'You'll have to call the doctor,' I said. I thought that would be a much better idea.

'It's no good,' said Jack slowly. 'Mum would turn her head to the wall.'

'Then there's only one thing for it,' said Amy, as if she understood Jack. She had that practical look that made Jack and me trust her.

'There is nothing else for it. We'll have to get the books back as soon as we can. We'll have to find the thief. There is nothing else we can do.'

5

First Clues

Amy took the lead and we followed on. It happened like that sometimes.

As she spoke, Jack looked at me and I looked at him. I knew we were thinking the same thing.

'You're right. We must get the books back,' said Jack.

He made us a cup of tea and we talked. Or at least I did. All about Yellowface crawling around and the danger we were in. At the end of it Amy said why didn't she look after Jack's mum while we chased Yellowface? That way she could tell her mother what she was doing. She knew her mother would approve.

'I once looked after my aunt,' she told us. 'I used to read her stories. My mum thought I was great!'

Jack nodded. 'When I was small the travellers

told us many stories. I'm sure my mum would like you to read to her.'

Jack made Mrs Dobbin a mug of camomile tea and put a big hunk of bread on a plate.

'You can take it in to her.'

'A sick person needs something delicate,' said Amy firmly, 'not a mug.'

She looked round the piles of junk and found a pretty cup and saucer. She washed them and poured the tea into the cup. She went on as she had begun.

'I don't want to hurt your feelings, Jack, but a great hunk of bread is not appealing. What about – what about bread and milk?'

It turned out to be just what Mrs Dobbin wanted. She smiled at Amy and said she would love her to help.

Jack ate the big hunk of bread in one go, then cut some more thick slices and gave me one. 'What about *your* mum then? Won't she go mad if you don't get home?'

I spread thick Marmite on to my thick slice. At home I was only allowed a thin scraping of Marmite on a thin slice of wholemeal bread. I liked eating with Jack.

'We're in luck,' I told him. 'Mum's about to decorate. When she decorates she can't see further than her paintbrush. It's out of sight, out of mind!'

I stuffed the bread into my mouth and spoke while I ate.

I slurped my tea and left the breadcrumbs on the table. It was my way of showing I was angry with my mother. I dreaded to think what the living-room would look like when she had finished with it. An operating room, I should think. I wiped my mouth with the back of my hand. 'That was great.' I scraped back my chair.

'Tonight we must think what to do. But first I want to hear more about that phone call from No. 23.'

Jack cut another hunk of bread. I had the feeling he hadn't eaten for hours. He looked brighter and smiled when Amy came back from the bedroom with an empty bowl. Amy smiled back.

'Your mother said it was just what she felt like. She even let me tidy the bed. Now she wants the story.'

'She isn't like that with everyone,' said Jack. He turned to me.

'About the phone call. I know I haven't much of a memory, but I don't forget addresses. It's work, see? I mustn't forget them. But something must have been wrong. When I knocked on No. 23 the lady said she didn't know anything about a clear-out. She said she was never going to move. She was beginning to get her house just as she wanted. She was about to paint her bathroom black. I think she felt sorry for me because she made me go in for a cup of tea and began to talk as if she wanted company. She even asked me to call her Rosie!'

'It's all phoney.' I told Jack. 'Besides, she has my mother for company. But it's important to know if she had the same voice as the person on the phone. Did you recognise her voice?'

'That was it,' said Jack. 'It *was* the same voice. I might forget everything else but I never forget voices.'

I stood up. 'There's something funny going on. Come to think of it, my mum says Rosie has funny friends. Not that that means a lot. My mum thinks half the world is funny – and that includes me. But it makes you wonder...'

I thought of Yellowface. 'I didn't tell you at the time, Jack. After you showed us the books and started reading with Amy, I saw Yellowface again. He was running round the side of the cottage.'

Jack stood up. 'Why didn't you tell me?'

'I thought it was my imagination working overtime.'

'I expect it was.'

'I don't know.'

I opened the kitchen door. 'I could find out more about Rosie,' I said as I went. 'I know my mother can't see beyond her paintbrush at the moment, but she may be able to help us. We have to begin somewhere.'

That evening things were not simple. Mum had already painted the living-room ceiling. There was paint in her hair. The big dust-sheet on the floor was full of white blobs. All this had put her into a bad mood. But I had no time to wait. I followed her into the kitchen and asked her about Rosie. She poked her paintbrush at me. 'Rosie Sanders? What do you want to know for?'

I told her about the break-in and how it happened when Jack was with Rosie.

'There might be a link.' Mum shook the brush hard and put it in a jar of turps.

'I don't want you going round there asking questions,' she said. That was typical of my mum. I had to do something to keep her sweet, so I began to wipe the draining-board for her.

'Do you know any of Rosie's funny friends, Mum?'

'Of course not.' She spoke as if I had insulted

her. 'That strange lot? Artists and dealers.'

She took off her overall and watched me working. 'I did once meet a dealer she knew. Shifty looking bloke with a wall eye and a limp.'

That was enough. I stopped wiping and went upstairs to look up 'dealer' and 'wall eye' in my dictionary. Just to make sure.

So that was it. A trader with staring eyes.

I took a notebook from my drawer and under the heading 'CLUES' I wrote it all down. I always write things down to make them clear. Not a bad start, I thought.

A little later on I went with Dad to get a takeaway. 'Are there any dealers at the Golf Club?' I asked.

He laughed. 'The place is full of them. Half of them do business up there. Now. What about Chicken Tikka and Special Fried Rice. Will that do?'

Perhaps we could snoop round the Golf Club. Perhaps we could phone Rosie Sanders. There wasn't much time and any action was better than none. I looked round as my dad ordered Chicken Tikka and Special Fried Rice. It looked to me as if nearly all the people in the queue were wall-eyed traders. Or maybe it was hunger that made them seem to squint with bulging eyes.

6

The Torn Note

The next day a lot happened at school. The Headmaster gave out a notice about a contest. For a while it took my mind off our book hunt. It was called the Heritage Competition and was organised by some green group. The prize was two weeks in Greece.

You had to write about something green and you could draw as well. Like everybody else I wanted to win. We always went to Cornwall for holidays because my mother hated to fly. If I won I could take Dad to Greece instead. We would have a good time, fishing and eating.

Jack wanted to win as well. He said a holiday would do his mum good.

'You never know,' I said, although we both knew he didn't have a chance.

'I would have written out the cure,' he said

The Torn Note

sadly, 'and drawn some herbs. As it is...' and he shrugged his shoulders.

'Don't worry,' I said, 'we're going to get those books back. I've got a clue.'

I told him about the wall-eyed dealer but he said it was a long shot. Perhaps we had better forget it. He sounded tired.

'If I win the contest, we'll go halves,' I said. 'I'm going to write about the bicycle. Green bicycle routes.'

That evening I would try to forget about Yellowface and Jack's mum and the missing books. I would put my mind on my green bicycle routes.

The next thing that happened was in English. We were reading from this Shakespeare play called *As You Like It*. Jack shut himself off. He simply didn't listen. Before long, he went to sleep and began to snore.

It was the last straw. Old Shark's teeth shook with anger. His teeth slid about as he shouted. Jack stirred just in time to hear his punishment.

'You'll stay behind tonight, Dobbin. Read the scene and write about it!'

'But I can't.'

'Oh yes, you can,' screamed Mr Barker. 'I'm in charge tonight and I'll make sure you are there.'

To make things worse, Amy's mum had her eye

33

on a bargain and needed Amy to talk it over after school. So that left me to call on Mrs Dobbin, chase up the dealers, interview Rosie Sanders, look out for Yellowface, keep my mum sweet and write a brilliant essay on green bicycle routes. It seemed quite a lot, even for me.

'The key's under the mat,' Jack told me on his way to detention. He smiled but he looked a bit like an animal in a trap. Everything was getting out of hand. Even his front garden. One rosemary bush seemed to have grown and now stood between me and the front door.

I took the key from under the mat.

'Cooee,' I shouted as I opened the door. The kitchen was just as I had left it last night.

'Cooee,' I called again as I knocked on the bedroom door.

'Come in,' said the soft voice.

'It's me,' I said. Mrs Dobbin looked very flushed. She was too ill to hide her dismay. I wasn't surprised. I didn't have a chance next to Amy.

'Amy had to be with her mother and poor old Jack's been kept in for snoring in class...I don't mind reading to you, Mrs Dobbin.'

'Kind of you,' she said, 'but don't bother. If you could make some tea.'

I nodded and hurried out. I wanted to make her

The Torn Note

bed and hoover the floor and tidy the table and dust the ornaments. It must have been my mother coming out in me. Heaven forbid, I thought as I broke off a hunk of fresh loaf.

I tiptoed back. 'Would you like bread and milk, Mrs Dobbin?'

She managed a smile. 'That would be nice.'

I found myself trying to do it even better than Amy. I cut the bread into small neat squares and added a little honey and just the right amount of hot milk. I made sure the water was boiling and poured it carefully over the tea. I found a little cloth and spread it on the old worn tin tray.

Let's face it. You can't get away from your mother's ways.

I took it in and Mrs Dobbin smiled at me again.

'Good friends, Jack has. More than I have,' she said, a little sadly. 'It's the people round here. They don't mingle.'

On my way out I decided to have a look in the shed again. After all, there might be a clue.

Jack had not been near the place. I picked up his dad's boots and put them back on the table. Then I collected broken bits of glass and pottery and put them in a cardboard box. Although there was such a mess I had the feeling the thief was not a vandal but was in a hurry as if he were afraid.

I found a children's book of fairy tales on the floor and picked it up. It looked as if Jack had been trying to read it. There were pictures on every page and the print was big.

I began to read it. I am like that with books. Anything will do.

It was all about a fairy princess who was going to a ball and fell in love with a young ragged carpenter who had come to mend a cupboard. I turned the pages to find the ball scene. The ladies were in fancy dresses and everybody wore masks, even the young carpenter. He wore a mask that made him look like a prince. He danced with the princess and nobody knew. The king wore an ugly mask that showed what he was really like. I stared at it for a long time because it reminded me of something. Of course! Yellowface. That was it! He didn't have a yellow face at all. He was a man in a mask!

I felt really excited and looked round for any other clues. Something the thief had left behind, something he might have dropped.

I was just giving up when I found a small torn piece of paper. There was some writing on it and it was not Jack's. It seemed to be part of an address. Underneath was a telephone number. I couldn't believe my luck. I stuffed the piece of paper in my pocket and hurried home.

7

The Yellow Mask

'I've been helping Mrs Dobbin,' I told my mother as I panted indoors.

'That's all right,' said Mum, who was peering at the ceiling. 'Another week, then everything will be back to normal.'

She looked at me with one eye as if that was a threat.

I went upstairs and took the torn note out of my pocket. I studied it hard. By now I considered myself quite an expert on handwriting. The letters sloped forward as if they were tumbling over each other. The numbers sloped forward as well. A person who writes easily but in a hurry, I thought. I wrote the number down in my notebook.

'Charlie,' called Mum up the stairs. 'Dad and I are getting a Chinese. What do you want?'

'Sweet and sour,' I shouted down. My mind was

on other things. I was thinking that I could try out the phone number when they were gone.

I went to the window and watched Dad drive the car smoothly out of the garage and into the road. Then I rushed downstairs and dialled the number.

The voice at the other end repeated it. She had an extra loud voice as if she were talking to an audience. I hadn't thought out what to say or how to say it. I found myself covering my mouth with my hand and making my voice deeper. I asked for Amy.

'Rosie here, not Amy,' said the loud voice.

My brain ticked over with the speed for which it is famous. 'Rosie Sanders?'

'Of course!'

I laughed. 'I meant Rosie and not Amy.'

I deepened my voice even more and went on to make up a speech about my friend Amy who had told me Rosie was an artist.

'I'm a dealer,' I explained. 'I'm collecting modern works.'

'I deal with Mr Bonham,' she replied in a rather proud voice. 'He's a personal friend. He takes all my stuff.'

'What a shame! Never mind. It was worth a try. So sorry to have bothered you.'

The Yellow Mask

When Mum and Dad came in with the Chinese I found myself still speaking in a rather deep voice.

My mum actually smiled, as if I was growing up at last.

'It happens every now and again,' I told her in my normal voice. Before all traces of her smile had vanished, I went on.

'I'll have to help Mrs Dobbin tomorrow. She's in a poor way.'

'Nice of you,' said Dad quickly, as if he thought it was my way of coping with the decorating. 'Get yourself a quarter-pounder while you're at it.' He felt in his pocket.

'Here you are. Get yourself two.'

He's dead generous, my dad. I know he remembers the last time, when we both nearly starved to death.

That evening I made an effort with my project so I could get Dad to Greece. I wrote all about green bicycle routes. I became so involved I even forgot Yellowface and the missing books. Maybe I had the answer to the world's transport problems under my pen.

The following morning Jack and Amy and I stood in a corner of the playing-field. I opened my notebook with some pride. I was already aware that I had definite gifts as a private eye. But instead of waiting on my words, Amy began to tell us what had happened when she went out with her mother. She spoke in a rush so I could not get a word in edgeways.

'You know my mother loves bargains. She had found a rug at a very cheap price. I put her off it so we went along to this antique shop that has lots of very old rugs hanging up. There was one we both really liked but it cost too much so we didn't go in. Guess what I saw in the window?'

'A cat,' I said. 'They always sit in those windows.'

'Don't be stupid,' said Jack. 'What did you see, Amy?'

'A yellow mask,' she said in triumph. 'With red-rimmed eyes. Just like you described, Charlie.'

'I knew it was a mask too,' I said, ready to tell them what I had been thinking.

'We should go along and see it,' said Jack. 'Would you mind staying with my mum, Amy. She really likes you.'

Amy smiled. 'Bonham,' she said, 'that was the name of the shop, the same as that boy in the sixth form I once went out with.'

Now it was my turn to tell Jack and Amy what had happened to me. I showed them what I had written down in the notebook.

The Yellow Mask

'Brilliant,' said Amy and turned to Jack.

'What about you? What happened in detention?'

'Shark's teeth went on as usual. He knows I can't read Shakespeare so I don't know why he bothers. But this time it was worse than ever. This time he made things look really bad. When he saw I had a blank page he said I ought to be in another school. He would arrange a meeting at the end of term. He said I had nothing to offer. Nothing at all. Then he read something from *As You Like It*. All about the whining schoolboy creeping to school. Shakespeare understood what it was like if *he* didn't. I wouldn't have minded reading that for myself.'

I was very angry. 'We'll show him,' I said and Amy nodded.

'We'll get you to read and it won't take for ever. And we'll get the books back first and get your mother well.'

'Thanks,' said Jack. 'What if we go to that antique shop after school? It won't take us long. I have my work to do but that can wait. The light stays good 'til 9 o'clock.'

I shook my head. 'No wonder you go to sleep in class.'

I no longer felt so pleased with myself. I did

nothing next to Jack. If I were in his shoes I would sleep all day.

After school Amy went to look after Mrs Dobbin while Jack and I set off for the shops. We didn't have far to go.

At first we saw nothing much in the window. There was an old desk that must have come out of the ark. In the wood names were dug out with a penknife. Mr Barker would have had a fit. There was an antique bookshelf with a few old books leaning against each other. I studied them carefully but there was no sign of Gerarde's Herball of 1597 or the handwritten notebook by Dr Hall. Not that I expected to see them in his window. But the mask must be there, unless someone had already bought it.

It was Jack who spotted it first. 'Over here,' he called.

There it was, behind a large chamber-pot. It was with other masks, one looking like a bird, another like a king. I stared hard at the yellow mask. I knew that this was the face I had seen through the kitchen window. I would never forget the red-rimmed eyes or the yellow skin.

'That's it!' I said, and wondered what to do next. We didn't want to put Mr Bonham on the alert. We didn't want to let him know we

The Yellow Mask

were interested.

'You keep out of it,' I said to Jack. 'If Mr Bonham *is* the thief he'll know you. I'll go in on my own.'

'Wait a bit,' said Jack. 'You've got to think first.'

'I could go in and snoop around,' I said. 'I could pretend I'm doing a school project.'

'What on?' said Jack.

'Masks. And you'd better get going in case he sees us through the window.'

We arranged to meet at McDonald's. I said I would buy Jack a quarter-pounder. I told him Dad had given me money. *He* didn't like seeing people starve to death.

Jack walked off and I opened the door of the antique shop. My heart beat fast. My mind went into overtime. I didn't fancy being tied up and kept in a dark hole for days and days while Dad tried to persuade Mum to pay the ransom!

8

YB

The shop was dark. Rugs were hanging from one wall. Another wall was covered with modern paintings. Rosie Sanders's!

Then I got another shock. I *knew* the person behind the counter! It was the sixth-former Amy had once gone out with. The one who wore glasses and played the violin in the Christmas concert. Bonham the swot.

'Watcha!'

'Hi!'

'Didn't know this was your shop.'

'My uncle's. I sometimes work for him after school.'

The phone rang somewhere. Bonham opened a door in the wall behind the counter and answered it briefly. 'No, he's not here. Don't know.'

I could hear a fierce loud voice on the other end.

He banged the phone down and came back. He seemed more interested in talking to me.

'Hope your uncle pays well,' I said, because I could think of nothing else.

'Mean as hell,' said Bonham coolly. 'Still, it pays for my fags.'

I couldn't believe my ears. I thought Bonham was one of those prissy people who did everything right.

'You must be rich to enter these doors,' he went on.

'It's mainly dealers who have enough money.'

'Dealers?' I said, to play for time.

'Yep. American dealers.'

'What sort of things are they looking for?'

Bonham shrugged his thin shoulders and turned down his mouth. 'Any old rubbish.'

'Like what?'

Bonham glared at Rosie Sanders's paintings.

'What about those masks?'

'Those?' Bonham moved over to the window. 'He picked them up in Italy. If you're thinking of buying one, think again, unless you've won the pools.'

'I want to know about them for a school

project,' I said.

'School!' said Bonham with such venom I couldn't believe my ears. I began to warm to him.

'I thought you liked school.'

'Up to Christmas I liked school,' said Bonham. 'Then I went off it. My father decided to leave home for a 22-year-old tart. When he went my uncle didn't lift a finger except to give me this job and hardly pay me anything. He gave nothing to my mother and she's his sister. She can't make ends meet while my uncle is as rich as they come. Old Mean Guts. School? I can't be bothered anymore.'

I couldn't deal with this so I went over to the masks and picked up the yellow one.

'Did this come from Italy too?'

Bonham nodded. 'My uncle likes that one. He's been keeping it at home. To frighten the neighbours, I should think. Not that he needs a mask to frighten anyone. Have you ever seen my uncle?'

'Nope,' I said, trying to speak like Bonham. I was beginning to suspect he hated his uncle as well as school. If so , he might help us.

'It's not just masks I'm doing for my school project,' I said. It's – it's – well – it's early medicine. You know, herbs and that sort of stuff.' I paused.

'I'm going to the library for that. I don't suppose

your uncle has any books?'

'Yep. He brought two in the other day.'

My heart leapt but I thought I had asked enough questions.

'I'll let you into a secret,' said Bonham. 'The books my uncle brought in are right up your street. One was a herbal, if you know what that means. A good first edition of Gerarde's Herbal. The other one was by Shakespeare's son-in-law, no less - the famous Dr John Hall. He married Shakespeare's eldest daughter Susanna.'

Bonham told me it was a great find. It might even have something about Shakespeare in it. It hadn't been seen for centuries, he said. Everyone thought it was lost.

Then he sneered and said, 'Anyone normal would have gone straight to the British Museum, wouldn't they? Not my uncle. He's out to make a fast buck, he is. He and his ghastly friend Rosie Sanders. He put the books straight in the safe. No one can get at them now. Waiting for the right dealer.'

I could hardly hide my excitement. 'How did he get hold of them?'

'Cunning old devil,' said Bonham, pulling a face. 'His awful friend Rosie had an old neighbour who found these two books in his loft. He showed them to her. She knew how valuable they were though the old man didn't. He held on to them because they were in the family. He lived alone and when he died some distant relation had the house cleared by that dumbo from school. What's his name?'

I didn't answer. I didn't like to hear anyone call Jack a dumbo. I suddenly hated Bonham and his father. And Rosie Sanders, for that matter.

Perhaps Bonham read my face because he clammed up suddenly. 'Anyway, those old books came into my uncle's hands.'

'How?'

'Beyond me,' said Bonham, but he didn't look me in the eye. Perhaps he felt he had said enough.

I wondered whether to tell Bonham everything. It might make him talk.

'The thing is...' I began, but Bonham cut in.

'The old man will be back soon. Do you mind keeping an eye on things while I have a fag. He never lets me smoke.'

'OK.'

No sooner had Bonham gone out to the back garden than the door clanged and his uncle came in.

He had a mean mouth, a lopsided stoop and thin brown hair that showed his scalp. I had a feeling I knew him. I had never seen his staring eyes before, but I had seen that lopsided stoop! It came to me in a flash. Who else but the man in the yellow mask? I clearly remembered the way he stood and ran.

Things were moving faster than I had dared to hope.

'Are you being served?' he asked me in a thin whining voice.

'Yes. We...'

To tell the truth, I was so amazed I was lost for words. I didn't dare mention the mask project just in case old Bonham put two and two together. As it was, he seemed to be giving me a funny look.

'I've come in to see my friend from school,' I said without thinking. After all, old Bonham wasn't to know that classes don't mix much in our school.

Mr Bonham looked round. 'Where is he, then?'

At that moment young Bonham came back. He reeked of fags and I gave him a warning look.

'I'm going now, YB.'

'YB' came into my head without thinking. I couldn't keep saying young Bonham to myself and I didn't know his first name.

'See you tomorrow, Charles,' said YB as I opened the door and the bell clanged in my ear like a warning.

I ran up the road to McDonald's. Jack was hanging around the window. He looked hungry.

I bought the quarter-pounders. As we ate I told him what I had found out with the help of YB.

Jack looked as if he only half believed me. He knows my imagination very well.

'It's dead true,' I told him, 'and all that stuff about Shakespeare's son-in-law is great. Now there's only one thing we have to do.'

'There's lots of things we have to do,' said Jack as if he was losing hope. He did not seem to understand what a find we had, or maybe he did not think it could be true. It seemed as if everything was getting him down. I tried to cheer him up.

'We're going to break into that safe somehow or other, Jack. As soon as possible.'

'That's illegal,' said Jack. 'I'm in enough trouble as it is.'

'I'll come up with something,' I told him. 'By tomorrow everything will be clear.'

9

Amy's Idea

The next day at break, YB strolled over to Jack, Amy and me, with his hands in his pockets.

'Watcha!'

'Hi!'

'Thanks for keeping my uncle off my back,' he said. He smiled at me and once more I had the feeling we could tell him everything. I asked Jack if that was all right. He said there was nothing to lose now, so we leaned against the school wall and I told YB the story from beginning to end.

To my surprise YB didn't seem shocked. 'That's just what I figured,' he said. 'Now listen to me because I can tell you a thing or two. It's time for me to unclamp my tongue. My uncle is in it up to his neck with Rosie Sanders. They are both out to make a fast buck.'

I was amazed that someone my mother knew

had turned out to be a crook.

'How do you know?'

'Overheard this phone call a bit ago. You see, I'd left my fags behind in the shop and I couldn't ask my uncle. I know he makes all his phone calls after shop hours so I crept back. I have my own key, you see. I was right. He was on the phone, talking loudly. But not to a dealer. He was talking to the one who phoned yesterday, that arty-crafty phoney, Rosie Sanders. Even on the phone you can hear her voice a mile away. From his comments I think she was telling him what to do. 'Spy on those –' Bonham stopped and turned to Jack, 'her words, not mine - those gyppos up the road and find the books. Those gyppos won't know anything about valuable texts, she said. Or words to that effect.'

'That arty-crafty idea of the mask was her idea,' he went on. 'They talked about it for a long time. She'd seen it in the window. Said it was enough to frighten off anyone.'

'You can say that again,' I said.

'She's just the sort to come up with an idea like that,' said YB. 'She was laughing as if it was some sort of a joke. Ha! Ha! Ha! Ha! Not that my uncle minded. If you knew my uncle like I do you would know he is just the sort to do anything for money.

Amy's Idea

Anything. In fact, the sooner he's wiped off this planet, the better!'

Jack sighed. 'Why didn't your uncle offer to buy the books from me? I didn't know they were valuable. He would have got them for next to nothing and it would have saved him a lot of trouble.'

'You haven't got the point,' said Bonham. 'When you're mega-mean you don't think of anything so simple. He didn't want to lose a penny except the price of a meal for Rosie Sanders.'

I decided to be bold. 'Can you fiddle the safe?' I asked YB.

He laughed. 'You must be out of your tiny mind. My uncle trusts no one. He keeps the code in his head.'

'Then it's too late,' said Jack as if he were giving up.

I knew what he was feeling. What with Bonham and Mr Barker at his heels it must seem as if the whole world were against him. As if everything were given to him only to be snatched away.

'Your uncle must have the safe code written down somewhere,' I said.

YB shrugged his shoulders. 'If I started poking around old Meanface would smell a rat and chuck me out. Then I would lose my job.'

Jack sighed again. Maybe he would agree to

go to the police now. But before I came out with it, I gave myself one more chance to come up with a brain-wave. I have been known to have great ideas at the last minute. We stood for a while in silence. But in the end it was not me who had the brain-wave. It was Amy.

'I have an idea,' she said.

YB looked at her as if it was unlikely to be a good one.

Amy took no notice. 'My mother. She likes you, Jack. She doesn't mind me being with you. I could tell her everything. I know she would understand and want to help us. We've always been like sisters. That's why we go around together. She likes antique shops and besides, she knows your uncle's shop, YB. I think she would agree to go and tell your uncle she is a friend of Rosie Sanders. She could say Rosie Sanders told her all about the books and where they came from and all about her idea of the arty-crafty mask. My mother could say Rosie Sanders had looked on it as a joke at first but now she was having second thoughts. She could tell your uncle he was guilty of two crimes: theft and character defamation.'

'What's character defamation?' asked Jack.

'Calling you names,' said Amy with feeling. 'My mother could say if he didn't give her the books to

Amy's Idea

return to her neighbour, Mrs Dobbin, she would go to the police. Straightaway.'

YB looked at Amy with his mouth wide open.

'Nice one!' he said. He even smiled at her.

'The way you're talking we could knock them both out in one go. My uncle is bound to give in. He's scared as well as mean. At the same time he will never ever sell Rosie Sanders's paintings again. That will improve the shop no end. Well done, Amy.'

'Well done,' I repeated. Amy did not react to the praise. She looked at Jack instead.

'Trust me,' she told him. 'I will tell my mother everything tonight. I know she wants us to go shopping tomorrow. I will get her to do it then.'

'Why are you so sure she will do it?' I asked.

'I'll let you into a secret,' said Amy. 'She's got her eye on a Bonham rug. If she challenges Mr Bonham she stands a better chance of getting that rug on the cheap.'

At that moment the bell rang and I went back to class feeling happy. It was good to see the sparkle in Jack's eyes again.

10

The Bargain

After school I went back with Jack. His mother asked for Amy. 'She makes me feel better,' she said.

We told her Amy was shopping and Mrs Dobbin sighed. She looked hot and unwell but she still would not have the doctor. It was Amy or nothing.

Jack was near to tears. He made his mother a cup of tea and settled her down to sleep.

I followed him outside to the shed. He picked up his dad's boots and put them in the right place.

'When you've got money from the books you'll be able to look for your dad.'

I don't know why I said that. It came out without my thinking. Jack sighed.

'He should be around to help. He knew a lot of cures. The only thing that can help now is the cure in the notebook.'

The Bargain

So that was it. That was why Jack was stuck on that cure as if it were magic. He was trying to be like his missing dad.

He picked up one boot and fiddled with the lace. 'If only I could have copied down that cure!'

'We'll have it by tomorrow evening,' I told him. 'Then you'll be able to help your mum. You might become rich and famous as well. It's not every day a notebook turns up that might solve the mystery of Shakespeare.'

'I didn't know there was a mystery about Shakespeare,' said Jack. He looked doubtful. His mind was on other things.

'Do you think Amy will get round her mum?'

'She's got round yours,' I said, 'so why shouldn't she get round hers?'

Jack was very quiet. After a while he said, 'If I can't do something right soon, my mum might give up on me.'

I was shocked. I couldn't believe my ears. As far as I was concerned Jack did everything right. And more. 'Why do you say that?'

He sighed again. 'Everyone is better than me. You have to face it. Even Amy's better than I am with my mum.'

'That's rubbish. Amy's gentle but she can't do half the things you can. She can't do the round for your mum. She can't look after the pony.'

Jack picked up the book of fairy stories. 'The other night when I couldn't read the cure I tried to read this. I couldn't even manage a kid's book.'

It was then I found myself shouting, 'You ARE going to read and write.'

I was surprised how fierce I sounded. But I could not bear Jack's misery. At that moment I wanted Jack to read and write more than anything else in the world. I took the book from him and found a story in it all about the Green Man. It might help Jack with his green project.

'We are going to start reading now,' I said, thumping the table so that the bits of pottery danced up and down. 'And I mean now.'

I had never spoken to Jack in that way before. Come to think of it, I had never spoken to anyone like that. I have been brought up to be seen and not heard. However, in Jack's shed I felt a different person. I felt I could be myself and think what I thought out loud.

As for Jack, he was surprised by the strength of my feelings. He sat down and waited for me to begin.

We'll sound the words, I thought; that's the way for Jack. He's good on sounds.

At first he went slowly, but as he got the hang of

The Bargain

it he went faster. He knew a lot of words already but had lost his confidence. Until now. Now he was unafraid. He knew I wouldn't laugh.

After a while we went indoors and Jack made some soup for his mum. He woke her up and told her she must eat it. He spoke firmly to her. She was quite surprised. She sat up quickly.

We had bread and cheese. We ate off the kitchen table as we always did. Jack took a big bottle of Coke from the fridge and we drank the lot. We drank while he read. Despite everything it was like a party...

The next day I called for Jack. He told me he had made his mum eat porridge. He was sure it was good for her. He had left her some bread and milk.

We ran towards school and stopped when Amy's big black car drew up.

Her mother opened the electric window. 'I'll park over there and we can have a talk.'

We got into the back of the car. 'How is your mother?' she asked Jack.

'A bit better this morning.'

'Amy can visit her after school,' said Mrs Ratnayata, 'and I will come with her, if that is all right. I used to be a nurse and I know all about natural medicine so I will not frighten her. Now, I will tell you about last evening.'

She had a soft firm voice that made you feel at home. We leaned forward and listened carefully.

'At first I didn't believe Amy. Then I began to see she was telling the truth and I was very angry. There is a lot of meanness about. A lot of foul play. I know that myself.'

She smiled at Jack as if they had something in common.

'That is why I decided to help you. That is why I did what Amy asked. Besides, I could see no harm in it. I did not mess around. I went straight up to Mr Bonham and told him I had a friend whom he also knew. Her name was Rosie Sanders. I said she told me how her old neighbour had died and had left some valuable books he had once shown her. She was appalled when some distant relative phoned Jack Dobbin to come and clear the house. He took everything including the books.'

Jack nodded. 'There was a lot of stuff that night.'

Mrs Ratnayata continued, 'I went straight for it. I told Mr Bonham I knew he and Rosie Sanders had plotted to steal the books from Jack Dobbin. I knew he had worn a mask – the yellow mask in the

The Bargain

window that was back on sale. I said Jack Dobbin was a friend of my daughter's. If he did not give me those books for Jack I would call the police. It was as simple as that.'

She laughed. 'I still had not finished with him. I pointed to the rug I wanted and I set my own price.'

Mrs Ratnayata laughed again. 'He played ball. He agreed. It was the best bargain I have ever made in all my life.'

'Mega-brilliant,' I said.

Mrs Ratnayata started the engine and drove us to school.

On the way Amy turned round and talked excitedly. 'The books are in the boot of the car, Jack. We will bring them to your house after school.'

11

Fame and Fortune

That day school went in a flash, and I mean in a flash. Someone set off a firework in the classroom when Mr Barker was taking the register. It came from Jack's direction and it set fire to Jack's exercise book. For a moment Mr Barker was stunned into silence and then all hell was let loose.

Whoever did it never owned up. Perhaps they wanted Jack to take the blame. And he did, loudly and clearly. He was suspended on the spot. When Jack said he was as surprised as Mr Barker, old Shark's teeth raised his fists. He told Jack to leave the classroom there and then.

After school I called on Jack. I told him I had gone to the Headmaster and said he had been framed.

Jack was calm again. He handed me a lump of bread and cheese. 'It doesn't matter. I had more time to look after my mum. I made her some nettle soup.'

Not long afterwards Amy and her mother arrived with the old box.

We put the books on the table and Jack found the translation in the notebook. He tried to read it.

'You need a few more lessons,' I told him. 'Even I can't read that handwriting.'

Jack gave the cure to Mrs Ratnayata. 'Would you help me make it up?'

She nodded and Jack put the books back into the box. He put the box under his bed then took us all in to see his mother.

She was sitting up in bed drinking her nettle soup from a bowl. She smiled at Amy and said she was pleased to meet her mother. Especially as they looked so alike. Mrs Ratnayata waited for her to finish the soup, then took the bowl from her and sat on the edge of the bed.

'I used to be a nurse,' she told her. 'I have always believed in natural medicines. If you like, I can help you.'

Mrs Dobbin smiled and Jack looked relieved. Mrs Ratnayata stood up and said, 'If that is all right with you, I will go on calling at this time until you are well...'

'I'm very grateful,' said Mrs Dobbin. 'The folks

round here don't have much to do with us, so I have to lean on Jack. He tells me he's left school.'

Amy's mother frowned and spoke to Jack. 'You have to go back to school. You must insist the firework was nothing to do with you.'

'Mr Barker wants to get rid of me,' said Jack.

'He has no right,' said Mrs Ratnayata.

'I'll take the books to the museum tomorrow,' said Jack, 'then I will go back to see the Head.'

Jack wanted to sell those books as soon as he could. Besides he might get no sleep, knowing they were under his bed.

That evening I went home to find my mother had stopped decorating. We even had roast beef and dumplings for supper.

I don't know if it was the meal or not, but that evening I felt inspired. I finished my essay on green bicycle routes and wrote it out as well as I could.

It was hardly surprising I won the Heritage prize. Dad was over the moon. He said I might become a writer when I grew up.

Perhaps it was midsummer magic that made a lot of other good things happen.

The museum said the books were a great find,

especially the lost notebook of Dr John Hall. They said the British Museum would offer Jack a lot of money. With his new-found fortune he wanted to take his mother to Greece. But she fancied Cornwall.

'You could take my mum with you,' I laughed, 'she loves Cornwall.'

The local paper wrote an article about Jack. There was even a photo of him, smiling by the rosemary bush. He became famous overnight. The Headmaster had him back and everyone in school read the article. Everyone, that is, except Mr Barker. He was still set on getting rid of Jack.

One morning near the end of term he read out Jack's report.

'Reading nil. Writing nil. Homework nil.' He stared at Jack stonily.

'You've got no brains.'

He spat out the words as if he was going to be sick. At that moment his teeth really did fall out. I was thrilled. Mr Barker picked them up and put them back. He was red with anger.

'No brains,' he shouted again to show he was not beaten.

For the first time the whole class rallied round Jack. His new-found fame made all the difference. A lot of hands went up, waving the article at Mr

Barker. Someone read it out and I put the boot in by pointing out that the notebook was a lost manuscript written by none other than Shakespeare's son-in-law. There might be a reference to Shakespeare. If so, Jack had done more for Shakespeare than anyone else in England.

It was a real coup. It was worth being at school that day, to see Mr Barker's face.

We had to put up with Shark's teeth but we never went near old Bonham again. The truth was we didn't want to rock the boat for YB. He'd become quite a friend, in his own way. Besides, we had other things to think about. Mrs Dobbin for a start. With Amy's mother looking after her she was starting to get better.

Then there were our holidays and our future.

Despite Mr Barker, Jack was going to stay on and take English. He now had a special interest in Shakespeare and was determined to read him one day. As for me, I kept thinking of the holiday in Greece. Fishing and eating. Who knows, perhaps one day I would earn my fame and fortune as a travel writer!